RAISING GOATS FOR BEGINNERS

Want to know how to raise goats? In this raising goats book most off, if not all the beginners goat raising questions will be answered. Learn how to raise goats to be happy and healthy.

ANGELA JENKINS

Contents

Introduction

In this to-the-point raising goats book you will learn the secrets how to raise goats the easy way. Learn how to breed goats, raise the babies, how to milk goats step by step, medical care and much more!

Introduction

Goats are considered to be "herd" animals which means that you will need to have at least another goat. Goats do not thrive well if they don't have the company of other goats.

You will also need a pasture so that they can have room to roam around. Goats need to have plenty of space. In order for them to live comfortably, they will need to reside in a rural area, such as a farm.

You have to be committed to raising and taking care of the goats. They are like children and they need attention. You will also need to have a back-up in the event you have to temporarily go away.

Goats will sometimes need to treatment by a veterinarian as they are prone to getting different diseases and illnesses. The goats will have to get vaccinations and preventative treatment to keep worms and parasites away.

When you are purchasing goats to raise, get them from a breeder who has a good track record of taking care of them. You will want to talk to them to see how they have been taking care of the goats.

If you like pets, then having a goat is an animal that could peek your interest. Before you start that journey, there are a few things that you need to know.

Disclaimer

This book has ben written for information purposes only. Every effort has been made to make this book as accurate as possible. This book should be used as a guide - not as the ultimate source. The purpose of this book is to educate. The author and the publisher does not warrant that the information contained in this book is fully complete and shall not be responsible for any errors or omissions. The author and publisher shall have neither liability nor responsibility to any person or entity with respect to any loss or damage caused or alleged to be caused directly or indirectly by this book.

General Information About Raising Goats

General Information About Raising Goats

As mentioned earlier, you will need more than one goat. Having just one will not work because they are used to being around other goats. To keep them from roaming around, you will need a pen to hold them. Get a mesh fence that is about four feet. It will be high enough where the goat can get over the fence, nor will they get their head caught inside.

You will have to put forth the effort if you want to raise goats. There is plenty that you will need to know before you take on the task of a whole new world

A buck is a male goat. There are three female goats (does) for one buck. Goats usually have no more than two kids every year. The kid is another name for a baby goat. There will be more female goats as the buck has relations with the female goats.

When a female goat is in heat, they will wag their tail and stay close to the buck if there is one nearby. The female goat makes more noise. During this time, they are not very hungry and they have a decreased production in milk.

The female goats are usually sexually active and fertile between September and March. They can be fertile up to three days. If the female goat has not mated with a buck by then, they will be fertile for three weeks. After they have mated, they can keep milk for no more than three years.

When a female goat is with child, their pregnancy (gestation) lasts about five months or 150 days.

When it's time for them to give birth, they will either have one goat. Or they may have twins or triplets. The birthing process is called "kidding". When they give birth, it is usually an easy process without many complications. If there are complications, they are very few.

The female goat consumes their placenta after birth because it contains nutrients they need to stay healthy. Eating their placenta also helps the control of their blood flow. Bucks who may be looking for them may not find them as easily because the scent of the female's birth is light.

After the kid is born, they will remain in a safe place. Their mother will go off for a while to feed. She will get the kid when she returns and starts to nurse.

Once they have finished that, they will start to produce milk. This is called freshening".

The female goat can produce six pounds of milk daily while she has milk in her system. The kid gets her milk until they can go on their own. That can take up to three months.

Female goats (does) can live up to about 12 years on an average span. Sometimes the female goats have a short life span due to giving birth. If the does stop breeding by the time they've turned 10 years old, they usually live longer than 12 years old. Over breeding your goat plays a huge rule to their life span.

Bucks don't live as long as the female goats. When they breed, they use a lot of energy. This takes so much out of them that they usually don't have the strength to get back in shape.

How To Tale Care Of A Newborn Goat

How To Take Care Of A Newborn Goat

A brand new goat has just been born to its nanny. This is the beginning of a new life for you and the newborn goat. There is plenty for you to do, starting with removing the wet and cold goo that they come into the world with.

The goat's head will be wrapped in a membrane and it may not be able to breathe at first. Unlike a regular human baby delivery, this is a normal process.

As with a human baby, the umbilical cord should be detached. If it does not do that with the newborn goat, use two pieces of thread and create a knot around the cord. Use a pair of sharp scissors to cut between the knots.

Clear the membranes by using a clean cloth or a towel.

You will usually find the membranes on their nose (nostrils) as well as their head. Take another clean cloth and wrap it around your hand. Place it inside the newborn's mouth to remove debris and mucous.

The goat has to be stimulated. Gently stroke the sides of the goat. This not only helps with stimulation, but it also helps to get their blood pumping. Soon afterwards, you will be able to hear them breathing. Keep the newborn warm and dry with clean towels.

Place a bulb syringe into their throat and suck out secretions or tissues that were left from before. Close one nostril by pinching it and place the syringe into the open nostril. Do the same thing with the other nostril.

If you don't have a bulb syringe, you can use a strand of clean hay into their nose. Make jiggling movements with the hay until the baby goat sneezes. Once they sneeze, any excess that was left should be gone from the nasal cavities.

Get a container and fill it will iodine solution (7%). Put the end of the goat's umbilical cord inside of the container. With the open end of the container, press it against the newborn's stomach and cover the entire area with the iodine with the exception of the newborn's genitals.

Take the teats of the nanny and squeeze them. You want to get rid of any obstructions and get milk to start coming out. Place the newborn (or kid) close to their mother. You are working on feeding them for the first time.

To get them adjusted, put a tiny bit of milk on the kid's lips. If they don't want it, give them a bottle. Once they feel like suckling from their mom, they will try again.

After they have been in the world for about an hour, the newborn should have no more than eight ounces of milk. After that, allow the mother to take care of their child.

Give the milk to the baby goat and place it in a small container. You will need to collect colostrum, which is the first milk that you will get from them. Baby goats need this because it helps to keep them healthy.

See if the baby goat has gotten accustomed to nursing from their mother. If not, the baby will have to be bottle fed four times every day. The goat's milk should always be fresh.

It is extremely important that your kid gets colostrum. This first milk has plenty of carbohydrates, proteins and nutrients that your kid will need in order to stay healthy. It also contains antibodies, which your kid will need for protection.

Since the kid's lining in their digestive system adjusts within a day after they are born, the antibodies are needed prior to the adjustments being made.

The baby goat should be fed regularly every day. They should be fed at least four times daily. Their stomachs are small and they need plenty of nutrients. They will be assured of regular feedings as long as they stay with their mother.

There may be times when you will have to bottle feed them. You can use a baby bottle and cut a small X in the tip of the nipple. They should always be fed goat's milk; however, raw cow's milk will suffice when goat's milk is not available.

With the latter, three tablespoons of corn syrup is needed for each gallon. In the event they are not used to cow's milk, be patient and let them get used to drinking it.

The baby goat should always sleep in a warm and dry area. Make sure there is enough covering to prevent the goat from being in the sun and the rain. Ensure that the area is not drafty. For their bedding, use straw.

You need to use a material that does not stick to your baby's coat. You may need a heat lamp if the baby goat was born in the early spring season or the late winter season. The heat lamp will keep the baby goat warm.

Give the milk to the baby goat and place it in a small container. You will need to collect colostrum, which is the first milk that you will get from them. Baby goats need this because it helps to keep them healthy.

This baby goat is a few days old and need to be bottle fed

Using a warm and damp cloth, clean the kid's face, ears and back legs every day. Look on the hooves for debris and remove it. Make their coat look good by using a soft brush.

Your baby goat can eat grass hay that is free from mold. Some good ones to use are Bermuda or Timothy. You can start feeding it to them after they have turned a week old. You will need to get a special hay rack just for them. They will be enough room for their heads to get to the feeder.

At about eight weeks, slowly get them to eat other goat food. The food is different and contains enough protein for them. Follow the instructions to find out how much they can consume.

Trim the hooves on your baby goat. If you need assistance doing this, check out some agricultural organizations such as the 4-H Club and the Future Farmers of America. They can give you help on what you need to do.

Trimming hooves is a process that is not to be rushed. It should be performed on a regular basis. Otherwise, the baby goat will suffer from health problems in the legs and rotting in their hooves.

Since goats can injure themselves unintentionally, it's best to remove the horns of the baby goat. This is called dehorning. Baby goats can also injure others if their horns are not removed. If this is your first time, get someone who is experienced in this to assist you.

Once the baby goat has turned three weeks old, they need to be vaccinated. At six weeks, they need to have a booster.

For the bucks that won't be bred, they should be neutered. Four weeks is the earliest that you can start the process. You can cut, band and castrate them. If this is your first goat that you're taking care of, you should band them.

This method is the easiest way for first timers to learn how to neuter their goats. A band castrator is used along with a rubber band to place in the scrotum area. The blood flow stops going to that area. Their testes are no longer functional and can be removed within two weeks.

Baby goats can get worms. Schedule time regularly to get rid of them. Some things you must do to prevent them from coming back include keeping the goat's living area clean, not to graze a lot and not to have a lot of goats in the same area.

3

How To Milk A Goat

How To Milk A Goat

• Give the goat a bucket of feed. Start rationing at ½ cup and add more at a slow pace. Keep going until you have gotten to the amount that you are supposed to be at.

• Place the goat's head in the milk stand. Or you can secure the goat in a corner and make them be still.

• Wash their udder using a mild bleach and soap mixture. Thoroughly dry the udder with a clean paper towel.

• Take your right thumb and your forefinger and create a ring around the teat. This should be done at the top where the udder is. Squeeze the top of the teat and the udder together.

Take your middle, ring and pinkie finger and squeeze the top part off. Using the teats, squirt out a few sprays of milk into a cup. Look at the milk to see if you find abnormalities such as stings or blood.

• If milk comes out then you are doing it right. If not, then you are doing it incorrectly. The top of the teat must be clinched. You also have to make sure you are giving the teat and the udder a firm squeeze.

• Repeat the process with your left hand. Continue to squeeze out milk until you can't get any more. However, if you think there is more in there, continue trying. You can even massage the udder to get more milk to come out.

• After you're done, spray the udder openings using beta dine. This prevents the doe from getting a disease or disorder. This also prevents bacteria from getting in the udder openings.

• The goat's milk can be stained with a coffee filter or a paper towel. Staining is when you remove particles such as debris, hair or dirt from the milk of the goat. Put the milk in ice water and allow it to chill.

• You will need to pasteurize the milk using a double boiler. Heat it at 165 degrees Fahrenheit for only 15 seconds. Remove it from the stove and place it back in the ice water.

Tips That You Can Use In Order To Get A Good Batch Of Goat's Milk:

• You should talk to your goat while you are milking him. Be nice to him and talk to him in a nice tone. The goat will know that you really care about him and will want to provide you with plenty of milk.

• Don't' feel like it's a burden when you are milking. You should enjoy doing this. Not only will you get more pleasure out of milking the cow, but you'll get what you need in the process.

• In order to get good milk, feed your goat plenty of hay that has a lot of protein in it.

• Make sure to feed your goat food with plenty of grains, roughage and mineral mix.

• The does should be separated from the bucks during the milking process. Otherwise, the milk will not have a good taste.

• In order to keep the milk fresh and tasty, chill it as soon as you can.

What Is Better Than A Glass Of Farm Fresh Goat's Milk?

4

Breeding Goats

Breeding Goats

Breeding a goat is something that you need to have time to do. You can't just do it once and think that magic will happen the first time around. This is a serious undertaking, and you have to be willing to take time and put in a lot of work to make it happen.

• Your doe must be capable of breeding. They must be in good shape and not be too skinny or too fat.

• Look for a buck that can be a potential breeding mate for the doe. See if you can find one that is compatible with the doe that you have.

Check to see if his mother and other female does that are related have good udders. The buck and the doe should be of the same breed. If you are unsure about how to go forward, ask some goat owners who have experience in breeding goats.

• There are two ways that goats are bred: natural breeding and artificial insemination. Natural breeding cost less and is more likely to get quicker results. Just make sure that the buck is suitable for the doe.
If you can't find a suitable buck, then the doe will have to be artificially inseminated. The latter method costs more and there is no guarantee that she will get pregnant.

Your breeding goats should be in good shape - not too skinny and not too fat.

• Both goats should be healthy and eating a well-balanced diet. They should also be in shape to do this. If it's done naturally, the process will take a lot out of them. Other things that should be done include getting rid of worms and trim their heels. They should be administered a booster shot about two months prior to the breeding process.

• You doe will go into heat and start wagging their tail and not wanting to eat. They will get restless and mount other goats. She will also allow other goats to mount her. Her behind will be red and she will experience a discharge of mucous from her vagina. They usually remain in heat for at least three weeks.

• At the beginning of the heat cycle, the doe should breed early. After they have reached the heat cycle, they will ovulate every 36 hours after the cycle has begun.

• Goats should breed until they turn 10 years old. After that, they should stop. It can add more years to their life. Those that breed after 10 years are subject to see their lives cut short. Breeding can take a lot out of a goat, hence the strongly recommended 10-year limit.

5

Pygmy Goats

Pygmy Goats

Pygmy goats are great pets that you can take care of on your property. You will need to have two. As you know by now, goats do not like to be alone. They like to be around other goats. These goats can also be used for getting milk and meat. The smaller they are, the easier they are to take care of.

Pygmy goats are great pets that you can take care of on your property.

Pygmy goats are originally from Africa. They came to the U.S. in the 1950s. They were originally used to get rid of weeds in the yard. Because they are friendly and playful, they become popular and more people wanted them as a pet.

These goats look like regular goats with the exception of their legs. They are sturdier and they are also shorter than regular goats. They get their horns removed just like other goats. Pygmy goats come in black and caramel colors. For the most part, you will find black ones that have black legs or ones that are just completely black all over.

A full grown pygmy goat usually weighs no more than 70 lbs. They are year round breeders and have many children that can weigh up to 4 lbs. each. They usually have between one to three kids.

These goats should be clean at all times and will not eat from dirty dishes. They prefer clean water. Keep the water away from the ground. These goats will eat roughage that consists of legume and sweet feed. When they are still babies, their bodies are not strong enough for them to eat this kind of food.

Pygmy goats help their owners a lot. They will eat weeds and leave the grass for other cattle on the ranch. They will also make noise if they spot a stranger on their property that could cause harm to the rest of the livestock.

Pygmy goats are cute animals and they are affectionate. You can rub and scratch their snouts. They can also be in the same company with dogs and cats.

Pygmy goats are cute animals and they are affectionate

Pygmy goats need to be fenced in. It should be five feet or more in order to keep out dogs or other predators who may roam around.

Make a platform for the goats the sleep on. You can use an old door to do this.

If they eat from hay feeders, install them away from the ground. Having the feeder elevated can keep the parasites away.

Feed them grain mix. You can make it or purchase it. They can also eat alfalfa supplement that has grain in it two times every day. If their food falls on the ground, they will not eat it.

The pygmy goats should get their hooves trimmed every four months.

If the pygmy goats are more than six months old, get the worms out of them. You can do this once a year.

Pygmy goats need boosters and vaccinations every year. Consult with your vet as to which ones they should receive.

Pygmy goats are active, so you have to provide them with a place to play as well as something to play with.

As with other goats, keep the pygmy goat's coat groomed at all times. They enjoy this process because they like to bond with their owners.

If you are taking care of two pygmy goats, you can house them in a dog house. However, you can always get something larger so that there will be plenty of room. Having a larger facility is also a good idea if there will be mating going on.

Pygmy goats can be milked and can provide up to a half-gallon of milk daily.

How To Feed Milk To Baby Pygmy Goats

Even though the female goat is responsible for feeding her baby, there may be times where you have to get involved. Sometimes the mother may be too sick and will not be able to take care of their offspring.

This is where you come in. The kids are required to be fed four times every day. After 10 days, you only feed them three times a day. After 8 weeks, they get fed only twice a day. Once they have been weaned, they get one bottle. Since this will be new for you, consult with the veterinarian to see what formula you should feed them.

Warm up the milk and put it in the bottle. You will also need towels while you're feeding the baby pygmy goat.

Rub a tiny bit of milk on the nipple of the bottle. You want the baby pygmy goat to know that it's food for them to eat.

Since the babies are small, you will have to kneel or site down on the ground.

The baby goat's eyes should be covered. Work on opening their mouth if it is closed. When placing the nipple in their mouth, hold their tongue down. Get your thumb out of the way.

As you are feeding the baby goat, keep the bottle tilted upwards. You may have drips of milk around the area. Use the towels to get it up.

Eventually, the baby goat will realize that there is nourishment in the bottle and you won't have to resort to covering their eyes anymore.

After three weeks, the baby pygmy goat will start on solid foods.

Here are some things to look for when you are feeding pygmy goats:

• They goats should always stand straight with their head up. If they don't they are subject to get colic or develop other health issues.

• If the goat is not hungry, don't force them to eat.

There are some other things of concern that you should contact your veterinarian about if you see them happening with your pygmy goat:

• Stops being active
• Hunching
• Drooping
• Contracts diarrhea
• They get wet
• High temperature
• Weight loss
• Coat looks bad
• Lice
• Worms

6

Nubian Goats

Nubian Goats

Nubian goats (Anglo-Nubians) are originally from North Africa and the Middle East. However, they were developed in England. They like to live in hot regions and can be used for meat and milk. Nubian goats are large for both females and males. The females weigh about 135 lbs. and the males weigh about 175 lbs.

You won't have many issues about taking care of these kinds of goats on your farm. However, you will still need to know what to do if you plan to take care of them.

Nubian goats should always have lots of clean water. The container that the water is in should always be clean as well. You can use a bucket or a trough to keep the water in. These goats can take in two to five gallons of water daily. If they are in a warm area they can probably drink more. Or if they are larger, they can also drink more water than what's recommended.

Nubian goats eat alfalfa and clover hay. Make sure that the hay is of good quality. They also consume goat feed that is concentrated. With this food, they should also have a loose mineral or salt mix.

Nubian goats need to have shelter, so you will have to build one for them. Make sure that this shelter has a roof to keep them from getting wet. They don't like to get wet and they can get sick if they have to stand in the rain. If you paint the shelter a certain color, use non-toxic paint. Goats like to chew on the material. So if you use non-toxic paint, it won't bother them.

Goat of the Nubian breed

The area where the Nubian goats are sheltered should be secured. This can help to keep them from leaving the premises and to keep away animals such as coyotes that can get in and harm them. The fencing should at least be four feet in length and use solid posts that won't easily come out of the ground.

Maintain the yard and shelter where the goat(s) reside. You must remove the manure and used bedding to change it out for clean ones. Keeping their area clean and healthy will help the goats from contracting illness or diseases. The old manure can also be used for fertilizer.

Nubian goats should have their hooves trimmed every three months to keep their feet from rotting. You can use a hoof trimmer and hoof file to do this.

Close-up of Nubian ibex (capra nubiana) in the desert

Get your Nubian goat vaccinated every year. Continuously be on the lookout for lice and worms that can make them ill.

Nubian goats don't like to be alone so you will need to have more than one goat for them.

During the winter season, give your goat warm water so that they will drink more of it.

In order to keep the flies away, use flytraps and fly strips that are not toxic. This is so that you can keep their area free of flies as much as possible. If flies come in contact with the goats, they can cause harm to them by way of illness.

Keep in mind that you may have to do the majority of the routine maintenance on the Nubian goats instead of the veterinarian.

7

Goat Diseases

Goat Diseases

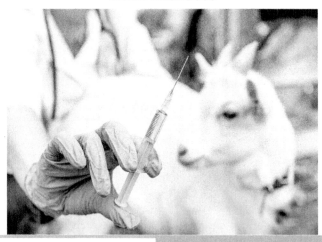

Treatment is imminent in order to get them well very quickly. There is a part that the farmer is required to play as far as getting their goats back to health. A lot of times, these diseases can be prevented if the farmer takes preventive steps to keep their goat healthy.

There are various diseases that goats will contract. Some of these diseases come from viruses, parasites and bacteria. The diagnosis of the diseases will vary. However, some of these diseases may be similar and can be difficult to pinpoint

Goat Conditions And Diseases

Abortion

Abortion in goats can happen between the 6th – 8th week of a doe's pregnancy. It can be caused by drinking water that has salmonella. The female goat can receive treatment from a veterinarian.

Anorexia

Can be caused by a lack of appetite.

Arthritis

Arthritis in a goat (baby) can be an infection in the navel. There is also arthritis that happens after birth, due to neglect of sufficient vitamins and minerals.

Anthrax

The goat gets a high temperature and doesn't have an appetite. They may only survive for a day. Keep the goat away from everyone. For the remaining goats, they should be vaccinated.

Bronchitis

If the goat gets a lung worm infection, they can get bronchitis. Get rid of the dust in the feed by putting more water in their mixture (regular or molasses water)

Bloat

Eating Lucerne hay can cause the goat to bloat. It will urinate a lot, walk funny and stomp their feet in irritation. Use hay that is dry when you are giving them fresh legumes. This can prevent them from bloat in the future. You can also put a little peanut oil on the feed.

Chlamydiosis

The symptoms for this are diarrhea and pneumonia. If the female goat is pregnant, they may lose their unborn child. If the child is born, they may contract arthritis. The goat can be treated with penicillin.

Coccdiosis

The goat will have low blood, diarrhea and feel week. If they are baby goats, they could die. They will need to be examined by a veterinarian.

Dermatitis

There are different kinds of this disease:

• Labial dermatitis – when milk residue remains on the mouth of kids that are pan fed, the skin gets hard and starts to crack. Their face looks disfigured. This can be treated with a cream.

• Labial and interdigital dermatitis – this happens when a goat eats plants such as ragwort Azaleas or they are attacked by mites. To treat this, use lanoline or petroleum jelly.

• Allergic dermatitis – this happens when a goat gets bitten by wasps or mosquitoes. This can be treated with a protective cream.

Eye Illnesses

• Conjunctivitis – this happens when a goat's eyes come in contact with grass, seeds, and thorns. The closer that they get to the cornea, the greater chance there is of contracting this. The eye area gets red and swollen. The affected area can be treated by using a saline solution.

• Pink eye – this is a contagious disease. You may see a discharge coming from the goat's eye. Wash the affected area with saline water. Use aerosol drops (2 drops) twice a day.

Foot and Mouth Disease

This disease affects young goats and adult goats. It affects the tongue, lips, cheeks and other oral areas. The adult goats look lethargic; the kids may not survive the disease. Keep them away from everyone else and get the rest of them vaccinated. For the ones who have the disease, wash their mouth using a mild disinfectant.

Foot Rot

This disease is contagious. It deals with various bacteria. The foot gets inflamed and it is moist. They turn red and start losing hair between their toes. The infection can mess up the horn of the foot. This can cause the goat to lose weight.

Goat Pox

The goat will have a fever and feel congested. If it's a baby goat, they will have a high temperature as well. They could also have lesions on their skin, but they usually don't live long enough for that to happen. Keep them away from everyone else. Wash the skin lesions using hydrogen peroxide. And warm water. Use antibiotic cream to keep out infection.

Hemorrhagic Septicemia

The goat will have difficult time breathing, a high fever, coughing and they may succumb to this disease. Treatment involves being vaccinated.

Hoof Trimming

In order to prevent the hooves to grow differently, they must be trimmed. Having them grow any kind of way will add pressure on the goat's legs. The pressure can lead to pain which would make it difficult for them to walk.

If some of the hooves have curled up, mud and other stuff can get inside. This can cause foot rot disease. Trimming is important so that the toe and the heel of the goat can be placed in proportion with one another. Make a schedule to have your goat's hooves trimmed every 90 days.

8

Additional Tips On How To Take Care Of Goats

Additional Tips On How To Take Care Of Goats

Find out as much information as you can about taking care of goats. Get some books, research online and find some people who have or who are currently raising and taking care of goats for a living.

Consult with more than one breeder. See which one would give you a good deal on a goat. Find out about vaccinations and other things you need to know before you seal the deal.

• Make preparations for your goat prior to purchasing one and bringing it home. They will need a secure shelter, water and food.

• From day one, you will have to put your best foot forward with taking care of your goat. Try to stick to the same daily schedule. Spend time with the goat so that they can get used to your presence.

• Have a regular schedule that involves preventive maintenance that includes hoof trimming and maintain their coat. Their coat should always be cleaned and well groomed.

• If you don't do anything else, always remember that goats are more content when they have company (other goats). They don't like to be alone.

• Do not breed the goats past ten years old. If you do, they won't live as long. The average life span is about 12 years, but some of them can live longer, up to 18 years.

This is because they stopped breeding when they were supposed to. Breeding can take a lot of energy out of a goat. By the time they decide to settle down, they don't have much energy left.

• When you put up fencing, make it so where the goat cannot easily access getting out. If you have easy access, the goat will be able to get out of the fence and roam elsewhere.

• If you have trees and bushes on your property, keep the goats away from them. They like trees and bushes. If they get near them, you won't have them much longer. You won't have to prune them yourself because they will do it for you.

• Don't give goats more hay that what they will eat. It is part of their makeup to eat less than what you give them. Study them to see how much they eat. Then you can adjust your portions accordingly.

• Don't be scared of your goat. There are times when they are aggressive. They will know when you are timid and can take advantage of that. Once they know that you can play their game, they will buckle down and act right.

A Healthy Goat Is A Happy Goat

Your first goat should be a female (doe) goat. They are easier to deal with than male (buck) goats. Male goats require more energy and more experience for you to handle. They can be aggressive; if the male is a billy goat, they tend to emit a strong odor that you may not be able to handle right away

Conclusion

Essentials To Always Have For Your Goats

• Always keep a clean and cool supply of water

• Always keep a clean and fresh supply of bedding; when it gets soiled,

change it immediately

• Keep a set of hoof clippers and a brush for regular foot maintenance

• Always keep a fresh supply of hay for them to eat

• Keep healthy treats on hand, such as fruit or vegetable peelings, corn, black oil sunflower seeds and various grains

• Make sure that the area for your goat is secured and fenced-in at all times; this can prevent them from running away as well as keeping out predators

Printed in Great Britain
by Amazon

80800278R00037